Writing & Thinking Skills:

PARAGRAPHS AND COMPOSITION

By Dorothy Rubin, Ph.D.
The College of New Jersey

Good Apple
A Division of Frank Schaffer Publications, Inc.

Editors: Lisa Schwimmer Marier, Kristin Eclov, Christine Hood
Book Design: RedLane Studio

 GOOD APPLE

A Division of Frank Schaffer Publications, Inc.
23740 Hawthorne Boulevard
Torrance, CA 90505-5927

GA13058

Contents

About This Resource

The ability to convey one's thoughts in writing is an essential skill, necessary for many aspects of our lives. Writing gives us a record of our thoughts, allowing us to stop to reflect, analyze, review, clarify, change, and understand better what we think. Learning about the writing process and how to write effectively is vital for all students.

Writing and Thinking Skills: Paragraphs and Composition is a valuable resource for parents and teachers. This book contains a wealth of challenging, stimulating, and necessary writing and thinking skills and strategies for upper-elementary and middle-grade students. The wide variety of materials will help parents and teachers as they work with students of all ability levels. This excellent resource is published in a format that includes practice pages that are easily reproducible for distribution in classrooms or at home, as well as Student Study Pages with essential information your students can use as a guide in their writing.

Whom This Resource Is For

The materials in *Writing and Thinking Skills: Paragraphs and Composition* are designed for students in approximately grades 5–8, but can be used with any students who need to improve their writing and thinking skills.

Recent national writing assessments have found that students appear to be gaining basic skills, though most still have difficulty demonstrating that they can apply these skills and use higher levels of thinking that involve analysis. This resource is aimed at upper-elementary and middle-school students because studies suggest that they are less likely to write on their own outside of school. *Writing and Thinking Skills: Paragraphs and Composition* will ensure parents and teachers that their students are gaining the writing and thinking skills they need. This book will help improve students' test scores, including standardized achievement tests, as well as teacher-generated tests.

Organization

Within the introductory material, you will find information about each stage of the writing process, as well as two valuable checklists for both you and your students to use as references. A revision checklist is provided to ask questions to help the creative improvement of the writing. The editing checklist asks questions concerning usage, sentence variety, capitalization, punctuation, and spelling. Use these lists as the basis to create your own checklist for your students to use as they write for different purposes.

The main body of this resource contains skill and strategy sections essential to students in order to write paragraphs and compositions effectively. Each skill and strategy section includes accompanying teaching material, learning objectives, special extension activities, Student Study Pages, and student practice sheets. The teaching material precedes the practices and contains the following:

Explanation
Learning Objectives
Directions for Student Study Pages and Student Practices
Extensions

The extension activities are intended to extend learning in each of the skill areas. You may use some or all of these activities as appropriate for your students.

An Assessment Tool Progress Report appears at the end of the book (page 106). This report can be copied and used for each skill area. The Student Study Pages and student practice pages are also reproducible. The teaching material offers suggestions for record keeping and can be especially helpful for student portfolios.

Reproducible Student Study Pages are provided for students to use throughout the unit. Students can keep these pages available for reference as they work through the unit activities and when they do their own writing.

The student practices for each skill are graduated in levels of difficulty. You can choose appropriate practices based on the ability level of each student. Clear and understandable directions are provided for student practices.

Teaching Suggestions

Writing and Thinking Skills: Paragraphs and Composition can be used in a number of ways. You can use the revising and editing checklists, as well as the diagnostic checklists that are provided at the end of this book, to determine the needs of your students. Of course, you can use these sections in any order that you feel is appropriate for your students.

The writing exercises in this series especially lend themselves to programs geared to helping students achieve more rigorous standards. The premise of this writing program is that most students can achieve at higher levels if they are provided with the proper teaching and help.

I encourage you to continuously assess your students' writing behavior. You can gain information about your students' writing by using observation and student portfolios as well as, when appropriate, informal and formal diagnostic measures. You then can use this data to either reinforce, supplement, enrich, or develop skill and strategy areas.

You are the decision maker. You must determine, based on the developmental levels of your students, which concepts and the amount of instruction that you need to provide.

7

The Writing Process

The writing process, which consists of a number of stages, refers to what we do when we are in the act of writing. That seems simple enough. However, when we attempt to analyze the writing process, we find that it is a complex thinking process analogous to problem solving.

Writing as a thinking act requires that we relate new information to our past experiences or existing information and that we analyze, synthesize, and evaluate this information so that we can present it in a coherent and logical manner. Writing as a thinking act requires time—time to mull over what we have written, dig deeper for greater understanding, create new ideas, destroy old ideas, explore our feelings, and evaluate as objectively as possible our creation.

When we recognize writing as a problem-solving process, we recognize that writing requires changes, rereading, rethinking, and rewriting. We understand that writing takes time, thinking, emotional involvement, and commitment to quality. The writing process consists of four major stages: *prewriting (or generating), drafting, revising,* and *editing.*

The **prewriting stage** consists of several steps before the actual writing. First, we begin with an area we would like to explore or write about. Next, we choose a topic and delimit it. Then, we must determine our audience (for whom we are writing). This will determine the design for our writing. After we have done this, we need to decide on our central theme, as well as our position on the subject. Next, we may need to discuss our views with someone or brainstorm some ideas, or we might want to do more research or reading about our topic.

Note that we have not yet begun the actual writing. Throughout our writing, we will continue to generate, analyze, organize, research, and recast our ideas.

We are now ready to begin writing. The **drafting stage** is when the writer puts down, in specific words, his or her ideas. As we already know, a good writer does not produce a finished, polished version at the first sitting or with the first draft.

In the **revising stage**, our writing is refined through thinking, writing, reading, critiquing, rewriting, rethinking, and so on; it concerns the creative improvement of the text. The writer makes changes, adds, deletes, reorganizes, and so forth, in order to say what he or she intends to say.

Finally, the writing reaches the **editing stage**, which focuses on the conventions of writing, including word choice and syntax, and the "fine tuning" of the work for a particular audience.

Special Note

Keep in mind that the writing of various drafts differs from the recopying of our writing. Some writers will go through a number of cycles of prewriting, drafting, and revising before they are satisfied that they have a draft to edit.

The Writing Process in Action

Prewriting Stage. Discuss the purpose of the writing assignment and who the students' audience will be. Brainstorm various topics they might like to write about. Help them choose a topic by modeling (thinking aloud) how you choose a topic. To choose their topics, students must keep in mind the audience for their writing, their knowledge of the topic, and the difficulty of the idea, as well as their own interest in the topic.

Do a mapping activity on a common topic students decide on, whereby you brainstorm words related to the topic. After the terms have been categorized and labeled, discuss them.

Next, have students gather information on the topic using various resource materials. Encourage them to discuss the information, analyze it, and finally decide on the point of view they want to take.

Drafting Stage. Now that students have decided on a topic, they can write their first drafts and so can you. Share with the class your first draft and explain your thoughts and ideas as you wrote. Explain how you tried to incorporate the central theme in your first paragraph and how you continually stopped to read and rethink what you wrote. Invite students to discuss what they did when they wrote their first drafts.

Revising Stage. Display your writing on an overhead projector so that students can see it. Then rewrite the draft "thinking out loud." Explain that when you reread what you had written, you realized that it did not say what you wanted, and it was not as clear as you thought it should be. You also realized that you did not have enough data to support your conclusions. Tell students that you need to do more research and reading on the topic. In addition, tell them that you are not correcting errors at this time, but rather concentrating on ideas presented in your paper. Explain that you will probably have to revise your writing a few times before it is the way you want it.

Ask students to revise their writing. Tell them that you are available for individual help and discussion for anyone who wants or needs it. After students spend time on their revisions, discuss with them what they did and what kinds of changes they made.

Editing Stage. Again, place your writing on the overhead projector. Have students help you correct spelling, usage, and other errors. "Think out loud" about how you need to change some sentence structure to create more sentence variety and make your paper more interesting to read.

Then, ask students to edit their own work. When they're finished, have them compare their first drafts with their final ones. When the project is completed, display students' writing. Throughout this process, meet individually with students to discuss their work.

Special Note

The writing process applies to what we as individuals do when we are involved in writing. Not all of us proceed in the same way. Some students will spend a great deal of time thinking about what they will write before writing it, whereas others may commit pencil to paper almost immediately.

Be aware of these individual writing styles. Know when to intervene, how to intervene, and how much intervention an individual needs. Help students recognize when to "let go" of their writing, as well as when they should continue to revise and "polish."

Now, let's look a little more closely at a scenario of two student writers to see the writing process in action.

Scenario

Andrew and Kathy are fifth graders in Mrs. Smith's class. They are fortunate to have Mrs. Smith because she is a dynamic, enthusiastic teacher who is as knowledgeable of her students as she is of her subject. When you walk into Mrs. Smith's classroom, you sense immediately that this is a room where exciting learning is taking place. Conspicuously displayed is a whole shelf of children's bound books that they have "published." Other books are also clearly visible, as well as several learning centers, children's art, and so on. What is most impressive to a visitor, however, is that when you walk into the classroom, no one notices you because each child is deeply immersed in what he or she is doing. The students in Mrs. Smith's class have been reading a number of fiction stories and books, and now they are going to write their own.

Prewriting Stage

Andrew has been interested in space travel for some time. As a matter of fact, his dream is to become an astronaut. There is almost no book on space travel in the school library that Andrew hasn't read, and the school librarian and Mrs. Smith have just ordered two new books for him "hot off the press." Andrew has no problem deciding what kind of fiction story he will write. It will be, of course, science fiction. Andrew is excited about his choice and discusses with Mrs. Smith some of his ideas. He also shares some of his thoughts with his friends. They, in turn, share some of their ideas with Andrew.

Kathy, however, is in a quandary because she can't decide on a topic. She hates to have to choose her own topic and isn't used to doing it. A transfer student from a school where the teachers always assigned the topic, Kathy has been in Mrs. Smith's class for only a few weeks. She will meet with Mrs. Smith for some help. Perhaps they can brainstorm some topics together.

Drafting Stage

Finally, Andrew decides that he has a good enough idea of the story he wants to write, so he decides to "give it a try." (This is not Andrew's first attempt at writing in Mrs. Smith's class—it's now the seventh month of the term, and students have been writing since the first day of class.) Andrew works for a concentrated period of time and seems oblivious to his surroundings. While he is working, no one interrupts him. Andrew only stops writing when the lunch bell rings. (Andrew surmises that it is about that time from the growls in his stomach.) Andrew is the kind of writer who likes to get everything down in his first draft.

Kathy, on the other hand, goes through her first draft very, very slowly because she doesn't like to keep revising and making new drafts. Kathy is more likely to think about and refine each sentence as she writes her first draft.

Andrew is so involved with his story that it is all he can talk about at lunch. If he has time during the day, he will try to get back to it. Kathy, however, says that she likes to mull things over. Anyway, there is something bothering her, and she doesn't know how to proceed. She discusses her problem with her friend Andrew, who makes a suggestion that she likes. She wants to think more about it, however.

By the next day, Andrew has finished his first draft. He worked on it at home because it was on his mind. Kathy does not complete her draft until the end of the week.

Revising Stage

Andrew rereads his first draft to himself rather than to Kathy, who is busy, because he is anxious to see how it holds together. He always likes to go over his material right away. Kathy, however, usually waits for a period of time before returning to her first draft. This gives her time to get away from her subject. Then she comes back to her work afresh. Andrew is reading his first draft to see whether he has to make any creative improvements to his story. In other words, he has to decide whether he needs to reorganize any of the material, and whether he needs to add, delete, or change anything. Because Andrew feels "stuck," he decides to meet with Mrs. Smith to discuss his story and ask for advice. Andrew does this, and, as usual, it pays off. Mrs. Smith listens carefully to what Andrew says. She takes her cues from him, and then asks some penetrating questions that help Andrew see his problem more clearly. (Before meeting with Mrs. Smith, Andrew knew that what he had wasn't exactly what he wanted, but he had not been able to get at the problem.)

Andrew now knows what revisions to make; he sits down to write another draft. Actually, Andrew writes two more drafts before he is finally pleased with his story. He also meets two more times with Mrs. Smith to discuss his story.

Editing Stage

When Andrew finally feels that he has the story exactly the way he wants it, he goes over his paper to check whether he has made any usage, punctuation, capitalization, or spelling errors. (This is the part that Andrew really dislikes.) Mrs. Smith wants the final copy to be as free from errors as possible. A paper or book filled with spelling, punctuation, and other such errors is not one that people enjoy reading, even if the ideas are excellent.

Kathy and Mrs. Smith have worked together to edit her material. Because Kathy does most of her revising as she writes, it has taken longer to work through her writing. Now, at the editing stage, Kathy checks for writing errors and confirms with Mrs. Smith that she is happy with her finished product.

When Mrs. Smith reads Andrew's paper, she suggests that he might want to use some other words for variety, and she also picks up some spelling, capitalization, and punctuation errors. In addition, she makes some suggestions about sentence structure. After Andrew makes these corrections, Mrs. Smith asks him how he feels about his story and whether he feels it is ready for publication. Andrew claims that he is happy with it and wants it to be published.

Special Note

Publishing is one outcome of the writing process. If students are involved in publishing their own books, stories, or a group magazine, they will have a purpose for writing, revising, and editing. The amount of revision that a student will do and the number of different drafts will depend on the student.

Revision and Editing Checklists

On the following pages, you will find two important checklists to use with your students' writing. The first, the Revision Checklist, concerns the creative improvement of the writing. The second, the Editing Checklist, concerns the final polishing of the writing. This second checklist is more extensive than the first. At the editing stage, the writer is concerned with having the most effective word choice and sentence structure to convey his or her message. The writer also wants text as free as possible from punctuation, capitalization, and spelling errors. Use these checklists as guides in working with students' writing, as well as to create your own checklist appropriate for your students. The amount of editing material listed on your group checklist depends on the individual differences of your students.

Revision Checklist

1. Does what you have written express what you want to say?

2. Should you add anything?

3. Should you delete some material?

4. Is your material well organized?

5. Is there a better way to organize your material?

6. Is there any new information or ideas that you feel you should incorporate in your writing?

7. Are you pleased with what you have written?

Editing Checklist

1. Did you check your spelling and look up any words you are not sure of in the dictionary?

2. Do you have periods at the end of your sentences that should have periods?

3. Do you have question marks at the end of your sentences that ask a question?

4. Do you have capital letters at the beginning of all your sentences?

5. Do you have capital letters at the beginning of all names and names of things?

6. Did you capitalize the word *I* whenever you used it?

7. Did you put in commas where you are listing lots of things?

8. Did you put apostrophes in the proper places in making contractions such as *can't, don't, isn't, hasn't,* and *I'm*?

9. Did you use apostrophes in the correct places in writing possessives such as *Charles's, Joneses', enemies',* and *deer's*?

10. Did you check for agreement of subject and verb?

11. Did you check that your pronouns (*she, he, it*) agree with the correct subjects?

12. Did you use active voice whenever possible?

13. Did you avoid the overuse of dashes, brackets, or parentheses?

14. Did you check for run-on sentences?

15. Did you use the proper verb tenses?

16. Are your sentences complete sentences?

17. Did you indent the first sentence of each paragraph?*

18. Did you avoid beginning all your sentences in the same way?

19. Did you use different types of sentences to express your ideas?

20. Did you avoid using sentences that are too wordy; that is, can you say the same thing in fewer words?

* Some writers use double spaces to indicate the beginning of a new paragraph rather than indenting the first sentence. The checklist should contain the form that students are required to follow.

Section 1

WRITING PARAGRAPHS

Explanation

A paragraph usually consists of a topic sentence, followed by a number of related sentences, and ending in a concluding statement. The topic sentence is generally the first or second sentence in the paragraph. The related sentences tell something about the topic sentence and are arranged in a logical order that makes sense.

Writing a paragraph entails:

- deciding on a topic.
- deciding on the main idea of the paragraph.
- deciding on a topic sentence.
- writing details that develop the main idea and are related to the topic sentence.
- using linking words to help give coherence and flow to the paragraph.
- writing a concluding sentence.
- revising and proofreading the paragraph.

The Main Idea

A paragraph is always written about something or someone. The something or someone is the topic of the paragraph. The writer is interested in telling his or her readers something about this topic. To find the main idea of a paragraph, students must determine what the topic of the paragraph is and what the author is trying to say about the topic that is special or unique. Once they have found these two things, they should have the main idea.

The Topic Sentence

The topic sentence contains the topic and states what the paragraph is about. It also usually gives clues to the development of the main idea of the paragraph. From the topic sentence, you can determine how the sentences that follow will supply supporting details—comparisons/contrasts, sequence of events, cause-and-effect situations, and so on—to support the main idea.

Special Notes

The topic sentence is usually the first sentence of a paragraph, but it is possible for any sentence in the paragraph to be the topic sentence.

Students should not confuse the topic sentence with the main idea. The topic sentence may or may not contain the main idea. If the topic sentence does not contain the main idea, it should help to anticipate the main idea. The topic sentence also usually helps to anticipate the development of the main idea.

Even though a topic sentence is stated fully and clearly in the paragraph, the main idea may not be explicitly stated.

Supporting Details

Details support, explain, or illustrate the main idea of a paragraph. They are facts that are essential to the main idea, and they furnish information about and give meaning to the main idea. Important or supporting details may be arranged in a number of different ways, depending on the writer's purposes. Usually, a writer uses a combination of methods. Here are examples of some ways in which a paragraph may be developed.

Sequence of events is used if the writer wishes to present something in some kind of order. It can be time order, stages, steps, and so on.

Supporting details may also be arranged by using **examples**. The writer states an idea and then illustrates and supports it with examples. When a writer uses this technique, he or she usually gives some clue in the topic sentence so that the reader expects examples to follow. For example, the writer might begin a paragraph with one of the following topic sentences:

Several stories have been told about Custer's last stand.
In a person's lifetime, he or she sees a number of different types of organisms.

In the first sentence, readers expect examples of some stories. In the second sentence, readers expect a list of the various organisms that a person sees in a lifetime. In these sentences, the words *several* and *a number of* signal that examples will follow.

Comparison/contrast is used when the author wants to show the similarities or differences of events, things, ideas, or situations. The writer may show both similarities and differences rather than one or the other. In explaining complex problems, an author especially may use comparison/contrast, as well as other methods of arranging details. For example:

Today there are a number of social scientists and psychologists who are raising chimpanzees in their homes with their own children. In one case, a psychologist compared the development of the chimpanzee with that of her own child. She found that at six months the chimpanzee was brighter than a human child of the same age. The chimpanzee seemed more alert and aware of her surroundings than the human child. Even at the age of two, the difference between the chimpanzee and the human child was not very great. Although the chimpanzee could not speak and the human child could, the chimpanzee had learned gestures, which she used to communicate with others around her.

In the above paragraph, the writer uses similarities and differences to present the supporting details. The similarities are the age of the child and the chimpanzee, the environment in which the chimpanzee and child live, and what is being tested. The differences are the two records of development.

Linking Words

One way to give a paragraph "flow" and order is to use linking words and phrases, such as *nevertheless, for example,* and *first.* However, these linking words, which give rhythm and sense to the sentence and the paragraph, do not have to begin every sentence.

Some common linking words and phrases include *first, before, then, next, after, now, hence, so, on the other hand, also, finally, perhaps, besides, moreover, however, therefore, nevertheless, for example, for the reason, unfortunately, fortunately, thus, as a result, in addition, in the meantime,* and *furthermore.* For example:

The day my dad came home and announced that he was being transferred was a turning point in my life. You can imagine how I felt. We had lived in the same town, on the same street, and in the same house all my life. As a result, everything was familiar to me. I knew every tree, every crack in the sidewalk, every bump in the road, and everything there was to know in a small town.

The Concluding Sentence

A good paragraph ends with a strong point, a conclusive statement, a restatement, or a question relating to what has come before. To end a paragraph, students should try to avoid terms such as *in conclusion, in ending,* or *to sum up.* Here is an example from *The Adventures of Tom Sawyer* by Mark Twain:

Tom Sawyer had found a new and weighty problem that was disturbing his mind. Becky Thatcher had stopped coming to school. He had struggled with his pride for a few days and tried to whistle her out of his thoughts, but he failed. He began to notice that he was hanging around her father's house at night and feeling miserable. Becky was ill. What if she should die!

Revising and Proofreading

Both revision and proofreading are needed for a "polished" paragraph. When revising something, students try to creatively improve an existing paper. When proofreading, students correct technical errors, such as punctuation errors, spelling errors, and capitalization errors. You may choose to provide copies of the Revision and Editing Checklists (pages 15 and 16) for students to use as they revise and proofread their writing.

Learning Objectives

Students should be able to:

- write the information they expect will follow from the given topic sentence, and state the topic of the topic sentence.
- write a topic sentence for each of the given topics.
- write a topic sentence for each of the paragraphs that is missing a topic sentence.
- write a paragraph that uses linking words and completes the incomplete topic sentence.
- arrange a group of sentences into a paragraph.
- write a concluding sentence for a given paragraph.
- write a paragraph using the given supporting details.
- write a paragraph on a given topic in which the details are arranged according to example, comparison/contrast, and some form of sequence.
- revise a given paragraph.
- proofread a given paragraph.

Directions for Student Study Pages and Practices

Use the student pages (pages 22–50) to help your students acquire, reinforce, and review writing paragraphs. Make copies of the reproducible Student Study Pages on pages 22–24 for each student. This section can be used for reference while students do the practices, as well as when they do their own writing.

Pick and choose the practices based on the needs and developmental levels of your students. Answers for the student practice pages are reproducible, so you may choose to give your students the practice pages, as well as the answer pages, to progress on their own. The answers are on pages 110–113.

Extensions

- In the editing process of the writing practices, encourage students to proofread each other's work. Do this in a positive atmosphere, explaining to students that it is sometimes difficult to see all errors plainly in one's own writing.

- Invite students to write a topic sentence on a small slip of paper. Place the slips in a hat or box and ask each student to pick a topic from the hat. Students then write a small paragraph using the topic sentence they chose.

- Divide the group into student pairs. Invite each pair to write a small positive paragraph about the other.

- Have students cut interesting paragraphs from news stories. Ask them to scramble their sentences and then exchange papers. Students can unscramble each other's paragraphs.

Student Study Pages

Writing Paragraphs

A **paragraph** usually consists of a topic sentence, followed by a number of related sentences, and ending with a concluding statement. The topic sentence is generally the first or second sentence in the paragraph. The supporting sentences tell something about the topic sentence and are arranged in a logical order that makes sense.

Writing a paragraph entails:

deciding on a topic.

deciding on the main idea of the paragraph.

deciding on a topic sentence.

writing details that develop the main idea.

using linking words to help the paragraph flow in a logical order.

writing a concluding sentence.

revising and proofreading the paragraph.

The Main Idea

A paragraph is always written about something or someone. The something or someone is the topic of the paragraph. The writer is interested in telling his or her readers something about the topic. To find the **main idea** of a paragraph, you must determine what the topic of the paragraph is and what the author is trying to say about the topic that is special or unique. Once you have found these two things, you should have the main idea.

The Topic Sentence

The **topic sentence** contains the topic and states what the paragraph is about. It also usually gives clues to the development of the main idea. From the topic sentence, you can determine how the sentences that follow will supply details, such as comparisons/contrasts, sequence of events, cause-and-effect situations, and so on, to support the main idea.

Special Notes

The topic sentence is usually the first sentence, but it is possible for any sentence in the paragraph to be the topic sentence.

Don't confuse the topic sentence with the main idea. The topic sentence may or may not contain the main idea. If the topic sentence does not contain the

Student Study Pages *continued*

main idea, it should help to anticipate the main idea. The topic sentence also usually helps to anticipate the development of the main idea.

Even though a topic sentence is stated fully in the paragraph, the main idea may not be fully stated.

Supporting Details

Supporting details explain, or illustrate, the main idea of a paragraph. They are facts that are essential to the main idea, and they furnish information about and give meaning to the main idea. Important or supporting details may be arranged in a number of different ways, depending on the writer's purposes. Usually, a writer uses a combination of methods. Here are examples of some ways in which a paragraph may be developed:

Sequence of events is used if the writer wishes to present something in some kind of order. It can be time order, stages, steps, and so on.

Supporting details may also be arranged by using **examples.** The writer states an idea and then illustrates and supports it with examples. When a writer uses this technique, he or she usually gives some clue in the topic sentence so that the reader expects examples to follow. For example, the writer might begin a paragraph with one of the following topic sentences:

Several stories have been told about Custer's last stand.
In a person's lifetime, he or she sees a number of different types of organisms.

In the first sentence, the readers expect examples of some stories. In the second sentence, readers expect a list of the various organisms a person sees in a lifetime. In these sentences, the words *several* and *a number of* signal that examples will follow.

Comparison/contrast is used when the author wants to show the similarities or differences of events, things, ideas, or situations. The writer may show both similarities and differences rather than one or the other.

Linking Words

One way to give a paragraph "flow" and order is to use linking words and phrases, such as *nevertheless, for example,* and *first.* However, these linking words, which give rhythm and sense to the sentence and the paragraph, do not have to begin every sentence.

Some common linking words and phrases include *first, before, then, next, after, now, hence, so, on the other hand, also, finally, perhaps, besides, moreover, however, therefore, nevertheless, for example, for the reason, unfortunately, fortunately, thus, as a result, in addition, in the meantime,* and *furthermore.*

Student Study Pages *continued*

The Concluding Sentence

A good paragraph ends with a strong point, a conclusive statement, a restatement, or a question relating to what has come before. To end a paragraph, try to avoid terms such as *in conclusion, in ending,* or *to sum up,* and so on.

Revising and Proofreading

Both revision and proofreading are needed for a "polished" paragraph. When revising something, try to creatively improve an existing paper. When proofreading, correct technical errors, such as punctuation errors, spelling errors, and capitalization errors. Use your revising and editing checklists to help you revise and proofread your work. Or refer to the combined revising and editing list below:

1. Did you check your spelling and look up any words you are not sure of in the dictionary?
2. Do you have periods at the ends of sentences that should have periods?
3. Do you have question marks at the ends of sentences that ask questions?
4. Do you have capital letters at the beginning of all of your sentences?
5. Do you have capital letters at the beginning of all names of persons and things?
6. Did you capitalize the word *I* whenever you used it?
7. Did you put in commas where you list lots of things?
8. Did you put apostrophes in the proper places in making contractions, such as *can't, don't, isn't, hasn't,* and *I'm*?
9. Did you use apostrophes in the correct places in writing possessives, such as *John's, children's, babies',* and *books'*?
10. Do all of your sentences make sense?
11. Is this the best way to present your ideas?
12. Does each of your paragraphs have one main idea?

Name_____

Practice 1

Directions: Read the following topic sentences and write what information you expect will follow in the paragraph. Then state the topic of the sentence. For example:

> *The effects of the earthquake were felt for a long time.*

The information that you expect will follow is reasons why the effects of the earthquake were felt for a long time or a description of the effects.

> **Topic:** *The effects of the earthquake.*

1. Living in a spaceship for three months was difficult.

_____

_____

Topic: _____

2. My best friend is always very lucky.

_____

_____

Topic: _____

3. No one could foresee the consequences of John's actions.

_____

_____

Topic: _____

4. Being the child of divorced parents can have its good moments and its bad ones.

_____

_____

Topic: _____

5. My first-grade teacher was the best teacher I ever had.

_____

_____

Topic: _____

Name _____

Practice 2

Directions: Write a topic sentence for each of the following topics. For example:

My First Airplane Ride
Topic sentence: *My first airplane ride was a terrifying experience.*

1. My Best Subject

_____

_____

2. My Best Friend

_____

_____

3. A Surprise Event

_____

_____

4. A Difficult Situation

_____

_____

5. My Most Frightening Experience

_____

_____

Name _____

Practice 3

Directions: Below are two paragraphs with missing topic sentences. Write a topic sentence for each paragraph. Remember: The topic sentence helps you anticipate events, and all of the sentences in the paragraph should be related to the topic sentence.

He was 18 feet tall and at least nine feet around the middle, and he had a tremendous appetite. He could kill a half-dozen cows and as many sheep and pigs, and he would carry them all home for one meal.

1. Topic sentence:

_____

_____

They tried hiding their farm animals, but then the giant Cormorant carried off the people themselves for food. So the countryfolk let him take their cattle as he pleased, for no one dared fight the 18-foot giant.

2. Topic sentence:

_____

_____

Name _____

Practice 4

Directions: Below are two paragraphs with missing topic sentences. Write a topic sentence for each paragraph. Remember: The topic sentence helps you anticipate events, and all of the sentences in the paragraph should be related to the topic sentence.

He took with him a dark lantern, a hunting horn, an axe, and a shovel. In the middle of the path that led to the giant's cave, Jack dug a pit 20 feet deep and 20 feet long. Then he covered the pit with branches and dirt. When the hole was thus cleverly hidden, Jack took out his horn, blew a loud blast, and then quickly hid behind a tree.

1. Topic sentence:

_____

_____

The countryfolk sang and danced for joy at the giant's death. They gave Jack a wonderful sword, and from then on he was known from one end of the country to the other as Jack the Giant Killer. Of course, with a name like that, Jack was the enemy of every evil giant alive.

2. Topic sentence:

_____

_____

© Good Apple GA13058

Name _____

Practice 5

Directions: Use the given incomplete topic sentence and the linking words or phrases to write a paragraph. Remember: A good paragraph should express one main idea; it usually has a topic sentence; and all the other sentences are related to the topic sentence. Also, linking words help give flow, unity, and rhythm to a paragraph.

Linking words and phrases: *first, then, next, perhaps, hence, so, on the other hand, also, finally, after, then, inside, moreover, however, therefore, nevertheless, for example, for the reason, thus, as a result, yet*

Incomplete topic sentence: The funniest thing that ever happened to me was . . .

_____

_____

_____

_____

_____

_____

_____

_____

_____

Name _____

Practice 6

Directions: Use the given incomplete topic sentence and the linking words or phrases to write a paragraph. Remember: A good paragraph should express one main idea; it usually has a topic sentence; and all the other sentences are related to the topic sentence. Also, linking words help give flow, unity, and rhythm to a paragraph.

Linking words and phrases: *first, then, next, perhaps, hence, so, on the other hand, also, finally, after, then, inside, moreover, however, therefore, nevertheless, for example, for the reason, thus, as a result, yet*

Incomplete topic sentence: The one thing that I especially don't like . . .

_____

_____

_____

_____

_____

_____

_____

_____

_____

_____

Name _____

Practice 7

Directions: Use the given incomplete topic sentence and linking words or phrases to write a paragraph.

Linking words and phrases: *first, then, next, perhaps, hence, so, on the other hand, also, finally, after, then, inside, moreover, however, therefore, nevertheless, for example, for the reason, thus, as a result, yet*

Incomplete topic sentence: If I were a machine, I'd choose to be a(n) . . .

_____

_____

_____

_____

_____

_____

_____

_____

_____

_____

Name _____

Practice 8

Directions: Choose a topic sentence from the sentences below. Then use the remaining sentences to create a paragraph that makes sense. List the numbers of the sentences in the order in which you arrange them, and then write the paragraph below.

1. They bossed me around, fussed over me, and never let me out of their sight.

2. At the time, I was quite mad at my mother for leaving me entirely in their care.

3. Therefore, I never got to play with anyone except them.

4. As a result, for the first five years of my life, the only males I ever saw were my father and the mail carrier.

5. Growing up as the only boy in a large family was no fun at all.

6. By the time I was born, my mother must have had enough of raising little children because she seemed to have given me up entirely to the care of my sisters.

Sentence order: _____

_____

_____

_____

_____

_____

_____

_____

_____

Name _____

Practice 9

Directions: Choose a topic sentence from the sentences below. Then use the remaining sentences to create a paragraph that makes sense. List the numbers of the sentences in the order in which you arrange them, and then write the paragraph below.

1. The spirit took off his own coat and gave it to the soldier, saying, "So long as you wear this coat, whenever you put your hand into the pocket, you will bring out a handful of money."

2. His decision was to defy death because he had so often done so before.

3. Then the spirit vanished.

4. "Also, because of this clothing, you will be called 'Bearskin,'" the spirit continued.

5. Then having stripped the bear of its skin, the spirit added, "This will serve you as a cloak and a bed as well, for you may have no other."

6. The soldier thought of the poverty to which he was reduced and knew the decision that he would make.

7. Therefore, he accepted the spirit's proposal.

Sentence order: _____

_____

_____

_____

_____

_____

_____

_____

Name _____

Practice 10

Directions: Following are three groups of sentences. Choose a topic sentence and then use the remaining sentences to create a paragraph that makes sense. List the numbers of the sentences in the order in which you arrange them, and then write the paragraph below.

Group I

1. However, he knew that it was just an impossible dream. 2. The more John thought about his situation, the more frustrated he became. 3. John started to miss practices. 4. He tried to practice more often, but felt he wasn't good enough. 5. Sure, he was athletic, but he thought he was too small. 6. John, more than anything else, wanted to be on the basketball team.

Sentence order: _____

_____

_____

_____

_____

_____

_____

_____

Group II

1. He decided that he would work hard to be the fastest basketball player the team ever had. 2. John decided that since he was too short for basketball, he would give it up. 3. The coach told John that he was pretty fast, and he needed someone fast on the team. 4. John decided to continue practicing. 5. But the coach at school thought differently.

reproducible

34

© Good Apple GA13058

Practice 10 *continued*

Sentence order: _____

_____

_____

_____

_____

Group III

1. His parents took turns practicing with him. 2. John may not be the tallest on the team, but he is going to be the fastest! 3. The more John practiced, the better he became. 4. John's older brother gave him a few tips. 5. The coach asked John to try out for the team. 6. Then the coach saw John practicing one day.

Sentence order: _____

_____

_____

_____

_____

_____

_____

_____

Name _____

Practice 11

Directions: Choose a topic sentence from the sentences below. Then use the remaining sentences to create a paragraph that makes sense. List the numbers of the sentences in the order in which you arrange them, and then write the paragraph below.

1. I hate using the one at school because it's always so noisy there.

2. All my friends did, but I didn't have one yet.

3. Then I walked into my room and there was a birthday surprise!

4. My mom and dad said there is one at school; therefore, I could use that one.

5. Yesterday was my birthday, but I didn't feel like celebrating.

6. Sure, he already had a really cool one.

7. For example, I'm 11 years old, and I still didn't have a computer.

8. What did I have to celebrate?

9. My dad kept saying, "Don't worry, you'll get a computer someday."

10. My dad gave me his cool computer!

Sentence order: _____

_____

_____

_____

_____

_____

_____

_____

Name _____

Practice 12

Directions: Here is a paragraph that is missing a concluding sentence. Write a concluding sentence for the paragraph.

Whenever my friend, her brother, and I would have to walk past a certain house in our neighborhood, we crossed the street and walked on the other side. The house, which has two monstrous lion statues in front of it, has been boarded up for as long as we can remember. Adults avoid talking about the "house," but when they do, they do so in hushed tones.

_____

_____

_____

_____

Name _____

Practice 13

Directions: Here is a paragraph that is missing a concluding sentence. Write a concluding sentence for the paragraph.

Tryouts are only one week away, but Jake still doesn't know whether he will be trying out for the hockey team. He really wants to be on the team, and he has practiced very hard for a long time. However, his brother's recent accident has complicated things. His brother got his skate caught on an opponent's hockey stick, which caused his brother to fall and break his leg. Now Jake's mother gets upset every time he mentions trying out for the team. Jake's brother is trying to convince his mother that his accident was just a fluke; however, he hasn't been able to do so. Because of her state of mind, Jake knows that neither one of his parents will sign the permission form that he needs to try out for the team.

_____

_____

_____

_____

Name _____

Practice 14

Directions: Here is a paragraph that is missing a concluding sentence. Write a concluding sentence for the paragraph.

One sunny morning at dawn, four of my friends and I went fishing. When we go fishing, we like to awaken while it's still dark in order to have an early start on all the other fishermen. The night before this trip, everyone slept at my house. Jason, Jake, Peter, John, and I all slept in our sleeping bags. We were so excited about the trip that we had difficulty sleeping. Actually, we stayed up until dawn. When it was time to go, the five of us attached the equipment we needed on our bikes and then went into the house to get the 15 sandwiches that my mother had made. (My mother had made enough sandwiches so that we would have three apiece.)

_____

_____

_____

_____

Name _____

Practice 15

Directions: Here is a paragraph that is missing a concluding sentence. Write a concluding sentence for the paragraph.

Whenever my friend, her sister, and I walked down the street, we always tried to avoid stepping on the cracks of the sidewalk. No one ever said that we shouldn't; we just didn't. Once my little sister, who likes to follow us, ran in front of us and purposely stepped on every crack in the sidewalk. Somehow my friend, her sister, and I felt that our luck changed after that. I know it's weird, but we couldn't seem to win one soccer game all summer long.

_____

_____

_____

_____

40

Name _____

Practice 16

Directions: Here is a topic and some supporting details about the topic. Write a paragraph on this topic by using the supporting details.

Topic: The uses of propaganda in television commercials.

Supporting details:

Propaganda techniques are used to get people to buy things.

There are a number of propaganda techniques.

The most often used technique is that of "getting on the bandwagon."

People don't like to feel that they are left out.

Television commercials try to make people feel left out if they don't buy a specific product.

_____

_____

_____

_____

_____

_____

_____

_____

Name _____

Practice 17

Directions: Here is a topic and some supporting details about the topic. Write a paragraph on this topic by using the supporting details.

Topic: Going to a new school.

Supporting Details:
> You don't know anyone.
> You are the outsider.
> Everyone seems to know everyone else.
> Everyone seems to be looking you over.
> You're afraid of doing or saying the wrong thing.
> You're always on guard.

_____

_____

_____

_____

_____

_____

_____

_____

_____

Name _____

Practice 18

Directions: Here is a topic and some supporting details about the topic. Write a paragraph on this topic by using the supporting details.

Topic: The effects of television commercials on young children.

Supporting details:
    Children pressure parents.
    Commercials mesmerize children.
    Products do not live up to commercials.
    Children become cynical.

_____

_____

_____

_____

_____

_____

_____

_____

© Good Apple GA13058 43 reproducible

Name _____

Practice 19

Directions: From previous exercises, you have learned that a good paragraph expresses one main idea. It usually has a topic sentence, and all the sentences are related to the topic sentence and help to develop the main idea. A good paragraph also ends with a strong concluding sentence. Linking words help give flow, unity, and rhythm to a paragraph. Use all this information to write a paragraph on the given topic, and arrange your supporting details according to examples.

Topic: Acts of courage.

_____

_____

_____

_____

_____

_____

_____

_____

_____

_____

44

Name _____

Practice 20

Directions: From previous exercises you have learned that a good paragraph expresses one main idea. It usually has a topic sentence, and all the sentences are related to the topic sentence and help to develop the main idea. A good paragraph also ends with a strong concluding sentence. Linking words help give flow, unity, and rhythm to a paragraph. Use all this information to write a paragraph on the given topic, and arrange your details by using comparison/contrast.

Topic: My two best friends.

_____

_____

_____

_____

_____

_____

_____

_____

_____

Name _____

Practice 21

Directions: From previous exercises you have learned that a good paragraph expresses one main idea. It usually has a topic sentence, and all the sentences are related to the topic sentence and help to develop the main idea. A good paragraph also ends with a strong concluding sentence. Linking words help give flow, unity, and rhythm to a paragraph. Use all this information to write a paragraph on the given topic, and arrange your details according to some form of sequence.

Topic: The earliest memories of my life.

_____

_____

_____

_____

_____

_____

_____

_____

_____

Name _____

Practice 22

Directions: This poorly written paragraph contains more than one main idea. Rewrite this paragraph so that it contains only one main idea.

In high school and in college, Brett's one goal was to be the best so that he could be in the Olympics. He practiced for hours every day. His family was unhappy about Brett's obsession to be in the Olympics. Brett's social life was more like a monk's than that of a star athlete. Brett's coach was a difficult man to please.

_____

_____

_____

_____

_____

_____

_____

_____

Name _____

Practice 23

Directions: Revise this poorly written paragraph. In revising, you may rearrange sentences, combine sentences, and so on.

Ben Simpson was all dressed up. He was all dressed up because he was going to a party. Ben was going to a birthday party for his friend Carol Anne. Ben had a great birthday gift for Carol Anne. Ben actually wanted the gift for himself, but he knew if he gave the gift to Carol Anne, he would be able to use it, too. It was a video game.

_____

_____

_____

_____

_____

_____

_____

_____

Name _____

Practice 24

Directions: Proofread the following paragraph.

Our english assignments are never very interesting ones. for example at the beginning of the term we write on how we spent our summer vacation, after winter break we write on how we spent our winter break. For mothers day we write on what is special about a member of our family. at the end of the Term we write on how we intend to spend our summer vacation i wonder how teacher's can be so unimaginative.

Name _____

Practice 25

Directions: Proofread the following paragraph.

The Pilgrim childs' life in school was'nt very easy. They usually had strict Teachers who were men. When chilren whispered in school he or she were severely punished. The punishment usually consisted of wearing the whispering stick. This was a peace of would that the child had to hold iside their mouth. There was a string at each end which was tied behind their neck. pilgrim children were also subjected to many whipings. I'am sure everyone is glad they are going to school today rather than a long time ago

WRITING A COMPOSITION

Explanation

To write a composition, students must be able to choose a topic that is neither too narrow nor too broad. They must be able to write a topic sentence for an opening paragraph so that readers will be prepared for what follows. They must also be able to combine paragraphs so that they are all related to the topic students have chosen, and they must be able to write a concluding paragraph.

Choosing a Topic

When choosing a topic for a composition, students should choose one about which they know something or about which they would like to learn more. Here are some questions that should help students choose a topic.

- What are my interests?
- Do I feel strongly about any special area?
- How am I special?
- What makes me different from everyone else?
- How do I feel about some of the major issues at school?
- How do I feel about some of the major issues in the community, city, state, or world?

After students have chosen a topic, help them understand that the topic must not be too broad or too narrow, and that they are treating a single subject. To help students understand this concept, write these sample topics on the board. These are too broad for a three- or four-page composition:

Transportation
Communication
Books
Sports

Point out that these topics are so broad that an individual could spend a lifetime studying each one. Show students how to narrow each topic:

Air travel
The television industry
Fiction books
Contact sports

Although these topics are narrower than the first topics, they are still very broad. Take the topic "The television industry" and narrow it into a manageable topic for a three- or four-page paper. Here are a few subtopics for "The television industry":

Production of television shows
Direction of television shows
Commercial television
Public television
Independent stations
Television performers
Television shows

Choose "Television shows" and state a few subtopics under it:

Comedy shows
News shows
Game shows
Sports shows
Adventure shows

Choose "Comedy shows" and narrow it down some more:

Situation comedy shows
Variety comedy shows
Comedy talk shows

Choose "Situation comedy shows" and narrow it down even more:

Family situation comedy shows
Adult situation comedy shows
Children's situation comedy shows

Point out to students that they now are beginning to see how broad the topic "The television industry" is. Each topic under "Situation comedy shows" is still too broad for a three-or four-page report. Show students how to limit "Family situation comedy shows" until it is neither too broad nor too narrow.

Manageable: *A Comparison of the Portrayal of the Parents in the _____ Show with the Portrayal of the Parents in the _____ Show*

Too narrow: *How I Feel About the Portrayal of _____ in the _____ Show*

Topic Sentence for the Opening Paragraph

The topic sentence in the first paragraph of a composition usually sets the stage for the rest of the paper. It is broader than the topic sentences in following paragraphs because it prepares the reader for what follows in the whole composition. The topic sentence of the opening paragraph should catch the reader's attention and make him or her want to read on. Here are two examples of excellent topic sentences. The first is from the *Autobiography of Eleanor Roosevelt,* the second is from *Try, Try Again* by Lilo Hess.

I was a shy, solemn child even at the age of two, and I am sure that even when I danced, I never smiled.

My life would have been entirely different if I had not met that mysterious stranger.

The Opening Paragraph

The opening paragraph in a composition is a very important one. It helps the reader determine whether he or she wants to continue reading. Explain to students that it introduces the reader to you and what you want to say, and it prepares the reader for the rest of the paper. Students should make their opening paragraph brief, to the point, and interesting. For example, write this paragraph on the board from "Would You Obey a Hitler?" in *Science Digest* by Jeanne Reinert:

Who looks in the mirror and sees a person ready and willing to inflict pain and suffering on another in his mercy? Even if he is commanded? All of our senses revolt against the idea.

Ask students if this paragraph captures their attention. Do they want to continue reading? Analyze what the writer has done.

- The paragraph is short and to the point.
- The central idea for the composition is contained in the paragraph so that the reader is prepared for what follows.
- The writer's technique of using questions gains our attention. (Notice that the questions are rhetorical; that is, they require or expect no response.)
- The writer tells us something about her feelings.

Special Note

We usually talk about the *main idea* of a paragraph and the *central idea* of a group of paragraphs.

The Concluding Paragraph

The concluding paragraph in a composition is very special because it pulls everything together. It should leave the reader with the main thought of the composition and with a feeling of completeness.

The following excerpt, from *First under the North Pole* by William R. Anderson, is an excellent example of a concluding paragraph.

> *Nautilus,* in one swift move, had opened up a new ocean for travel by atomic-powered submarines, an ocean providing a shortcut between many of the world's great ports. Mankind's dream of five centuries had been fulfilled. Thanks to atomic power the true Northwest Passage had been blazed—blazed in 1958 by 116 men in a magnificent ship named the *Nautilus.*

Special Note

Students should try to avoid using phrases such as *in conclusion, in sum, finally,* or *and so on* to begin the concluding paragraph. These phrases take away from the creativity of the paragraph and do not add anything significant.

Putting It Together

The following checklist and example for writing a composition should help students. Students should check whether they have:

- a limited topic that concerns one subject.
- a central idea for their topic.
- a topic sentence for the composition, which is usually presented in the first paragraph, and which may not contain the central idea of the composition.
- a list of all the points they want to make concerning their central idea.
- organized their list into several main topics that are equal in importance.
- divided main topics into subtopics.

The length of students' papers will determine the number of subtopics and details that they include. See Section 3: Outlining on page 86.

Example:

Topic: Air pollution.

Central idea: Air pollution is a growing problem that is largely overlooked.

Author's feelings: More should be done about controlling air pollution.

List of possible items to discuss:

Why is air pollution overlooked?

Cause of air pollution

Examples of air pollution

Areas that have a great amount of air pollution

Studies done on air pollution

Individuals' attempts to combat air pollution

People's feelings toward spending money to control air pollution

What is being done about air pollution?

What can be done about air pollution?

Consequences from not controlling air pollution

WRITING A COMPOSITION

Letter Writing

Most people enjoy receiving letters. Many times, in order to receive a letter, one must write a letter. The **friendly letter** is one students will probably write most often.

Heading: The heading may give the writer's address and the date, or merely the date.

Greeting: The greeting is a way of saying "hello" and states to whom you are writing the letter.

Body: The body is the major part of the letter. It presents your message.

Closing: The closing is a way of saying goodbye.

Signature: The signature tells the person receiving the letter who wrote it. In a friendly letter, usually only the first name is given.

The **business letter** is similar in most respects to the friendly letter; however, it is more formal, more information is usually given, and it also includes an inside address. The parts of a business letter follow:

Heading: The heading includes the writer's address and the date.

Inside address: The inside address includes the title of the person to whom the letter is being sent and his or her address.

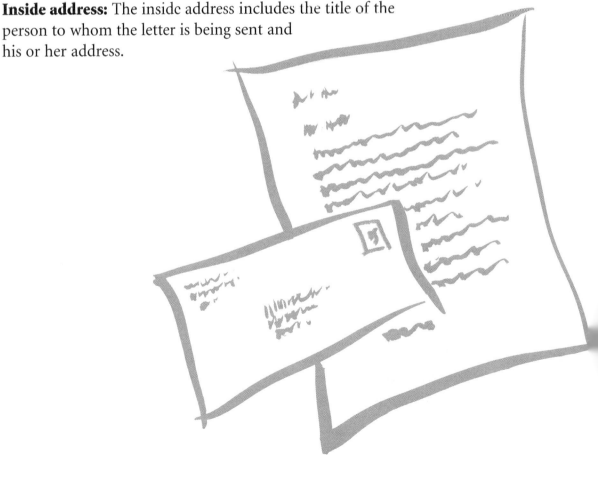

Greeting: The greeting is more formal in a business letter than in a friendly letter. The greeting includes the name and title of the person receiving the letter. If the name or title of the person is not known, the person may be addressed in the greeting as *Dear Sir* or *Dear Madam*. The greeting, which is followed by a colon (:), is placed below the inside address.

Body: The body of a business letter, like the body of a friendly letter, contains the message and is the main part of the letter. However, the body of a business letter is written more formally.

Closing: The closing of a business letter is more formal than the closing of a friendly letter. The most common closings are *Sincerely yours, Sincerely, Yours truly,* or *Cordially.* The closing is followed by a comma (,).

Signature: The signature of a business letter is more formal than that of a friendly letter. It usually includes your whole name, and it is handwritten. The signature is below the closing.

Special Notes

Business letters today are mostly written with the two addresses, the closing, and the signature flush left. Friendly letters may also be written in the same way. In most friendly letters, however, the first sentence of each paragraph is indented and the closing and signature are placed under the date to the right. In a typed business letter, the typed name is usually below the handwritten signature.

It is very important that students correctly address the envelope in their letters as well. The envelope should always have a return address. The return address is usually placed in the upper left-hand corner. The return address should include the name and address of the writer. In the center of the envelope, remind students to write the complete address of the person to whom they are writing.

Learning Objectives

Students should be able to:

- determine whether a topic is too broad, too narrow, or manageable.
- enlarge topics that are too narrow.
- narrow topics that are too broad.
- choose the sentence that would make the best topic sentence for a given topic.
- write a topic sentence for the first paragraph in a composition on a given topic.
- write an introductory paragraph for a composition concerning their childhood and choose a title for it.

- write an introductory paragraph for a composition on a given topic.
- write a concluding paragraph for a composition on a given topic.
- write a concluding paragraph for a composition concerning their childhood.
- choose a topic, limit the topic, state a central idea for it, state feelings about it, and list some possible items to discuss.
- choose a topic, state a central idea for it, state feelings about it, list some possible items to discuss, organize the items, and write the composition.
- write a friendly letter.
- write a thank-you letter.
- write an informal invitation.
- write a business letter.

Directions for Student Study Pages and Practices

Use the student pages (pages 60–85) to help your students acquire, reinforce, and review writing a composition or letter. Make copies of the reproducible Student Study Pages on pages 60–66 for each student. This section can be used as reference while they do the student practices and when they do their own writing.

Pick and choose the practices based on the needs and developmental levels of your students. Answers for the student practice pages are reproducible, so you may choose to give students the practice pages as well as the answer pages to progress on their own. The answers are on pages 113–115.

Extensions

- Divide the group into teams. Then write very broad topics on the board or on chart paper. Assign a topic to each team, and ask each team to come up with as many ways to narrow the topic as they can in a given amount of time.
- Write concluding sentences on slips of paper. Students choose a slip and write a paragraph to match the concluding sentence.

WRITING A COMPOSITION

- Discuss with students some ideas or suggestions they would like to see put into action in their school or community. Then, as a group, write a business letter to the proper authorities. Or, you may want to organize an Earth Day celebration or Cleanup Day for your community. Students can write a business letter requesting permission to organize this special day at their school.

Student Study Pages

Writing a Composition

To write a **composition**, choose a topic that is neither too broad nor too narrow. Write a topic sentence for an opening paragraph of a composition so that readers will be prepared for what follows. Combine the paragraphs so that they are all related to the topic you have chosen, and then write a concluding paragraph.

Choosing a Topic

When choosing a topic for a composition, choose one that you know something about or one about which you would like to learn more. Here are some questions that should help you choose a topic:

- What are my interests?
- Do I feel strongly about any special area?
- How am I special?
- What makes me different from everyone else?
- How do I feel about some of the major issues at school?
- How do I feel about some of the major issues in the community, city, state, or world?

After you have chosen a topic, make certain that it is neither too broad nor too narrow and that you are treating a single subject.

Topic Sentence for the Opening Paragraph

The **topic sentence** in the first paragraph of a composition usually sets the stage for the rest of the paper. It is broader than the topic sentences in following paragraphs because it prepares the reader for what follows in the whole composition. The topic sentence of the opening paragraph should catch the reader's attention and make him or her want to read on.

The Opening Paragraph

The **opening paragraph** in your composition is a very important one. It helps the reader determine whether he or she wants to continue reading. It introduces the reader to you and what you want to say, and it prepares the reader for the rest of your paper. Make your opening paragraph brief, to the point, and interesting. Make sure that:

- the paragraph is short and to the point.
- the topic sentence for the composition is contained in the paragraph so that the reader is prepared for what follows.

60

Student Study Pages *continued*

■ the paragraph tells something about your feelings.

Special Note

We usually talk about the *main idea* of a paragraph and the *central idea* of a group of paragraphs.

The Concluding Paragraph

The concluding paragraph in your composition is very special because it pulls everything in your composition together. It should leave your reader with the main thought of the composition and with a feeling of completeness.

Special Note

Try to avoid using phrases such as *in conclusion, in sum, finally,* or *and so on* to begin your concluding paragraph. These phrases take away from the creativity of your paragraph and do not add anything significant to it.

Putting It Together

When writing a composition, you must first have a limited topic that concerns one subject. Next, you must develop a central idea for your topic. The central idea is usually presented in your first paragraph, and all other paragraphs should develop this central idea.

To help you in writing your composition, you should, after you have your central idea, make a list of all the points you want to make concerning your central idea. You can then organize your list into several main topics that are equal in importance. After you have organized your main topics, you can divide them into subtopics. (The length of your paper will determine the number of subtopics and details that you include.)

The following checklist and example for writing a composition should help you. You should have:

■ a limited topic that concerns one subject.

■ a central idea for your topic.

■ a topic sentence for the composition, which is usually presented in the first paragraph, and which may or may not contain the central idea.

Student Study Pages *continued*

- a list of all the points you want to make concerning your central idea.
- organized your list into several main topics that are equal in importance.
- divided main topics into subtopics. (The length of your paper will determine the number of subtopics and details you include.)

Below are a topic, central idea, author's feelings, and a short composition. Notice how all of the paragraphs develop the central idea of the composition. The comments to the left of each paragraph will help you observe how each paragraph is related to the next, so that there is flow, order, and continuity in the composition.

Topic: The everyday wonders of nature.

Central idea: We should become aware of the everyday wondrous phenomena of nature that are all around us.

Author's feelings: We should not only become more aware of the beauty of nature, but also of its utility.

Paragraph 1: Topic Sentence

The topic sentence in the introductory paragraph prepares the reader for what follows. It is broader than the topic sentences in the other paragraphs. It gives the reader the writer's feelings about the topic and some information as to what the composition is about.

Paragraph 1: Opening Paragraph

The opening paragraph should be interestingly written to attract the reader's attention; it should introduce the reader to the topic; and it should prepare the reader for the rest of the paper. Notice how the topic sentence prepares the reader for examples of wondrous phenomena, and notice how the last sentence is a question that pulls the examples of the paragraph together.

Wondrous phenomena of nature are all around us, and we should become more aware of these. For example, have you ever awakened early to watch the sun rise? Have you ever stopped to observe a setting sun, a star-filled sky, or an October moon? Have you ever gone out after a rainfall and delighted in the scent of the fresh air? Have you taken time to listen to the songs of the birds, the trees rustling in the wind, or the music of the crickets? Have you ever held a seashell to your ear and heard the roar of the ocean? Have you tasted fresh berries, melon, or spring water? Have you ever had any of the above experiences? Have you ever marveled at the beauty of it all?

Do you realize that rock is one of nature's wonders? For example, most of us have seen rocks, touched them, and played with them, but have you discovered the beauty and uses of rocks? One way

Student Study Pages *continued*

Paragraph 2:

Notice that the topic sentence is more specific than that of the introductory paragraph. Notice also that the topic sentence prepares you for the examples that follow. This paragraph discusses the beauty of rocks and ends with a suggestion.

Paragraph 3:

This paragraph is a follow-up to paragraph two. It continues the discussion on rocks and describes some of their uses.

Paragraph 4:

This paragraph is still focused on rocks. In this paragraph, an example of the usefulness of mountains (large rock formations) is given.

Paragraph 5:

This paragraph starts a new example of the wonders of nature. The topic sentence of the paragraph prepares the reader for a discussion of soil and rain as necessary for life.

Paragraph 6:
Concluding Paragraph

The concluding paragraph emphasizes the central idea of the article, and it again presents the author's feelings. It leaves the reader with a feeling of completeness. Notice that such terms as in summary, in conclusion, *and* finally *are not used.*

to do this is to collect a variety of hard rocks. Choose one and start rubbing it with a special polishing cloth. Since rocks are minerals, strains of different colors as well as different shades of gray can be seen after they have been polished. Marble, which is an especially beautiful rock, is used for decoration throughout the world. Perhaps you can visit a building that has marble floors, walls, or columns.

Rocks are not only beautiful, but useful. They supply us with precious minerals, and they serve as foundations for all of our large structures. In some areas of the world, people use rock to build their houses. Crushed rock is also used as the beds of roadways and driveways.

Mountains are very large rock formations. Did you know that the snow-topped mountains are the sources of our rivers and streams? When the snow melts, the water flows down and supplies fresh water to our rivers and streams.

Some other wonders of nature without which we could not survive are soil and rain. Most plant life grows in some form of soil, and soil is not only necessary for food, but also helps control floods. During a time of heavy rain or snow, plants help absorb moisture by acting like sponges. Rain is also vital to life. Without rain, plants and animals would die of thirst.

All of us should try to become more sensitive to the wonders of nature around us. Nature has many things to offer. We should be grateful for this and begin to appreciate, respect, understand, and enjoy the environment in which we live. This can be an exciting adventure for all of us who are willing to explore and use our senses of touch, taste, smell, sight, and hearing.

Student Study Pages *continued*

Letter Writing

Most people enjoy receiving letters. Many times, in order to receive a letter, you must write a letter. The **friendly letter** is the one you will probably write most often. The parts of the friendly letter are:

Heading: The heading may give the writer's address and the date, or merely the date.

Greeting: The greeting is a way of saying "hello" and states to whom you are writing the letter.

Body: The body is the major part of the letter. It presents your message.

Closing: The closing is a way of saying goodbye.

Signature: The signature tells the person receiving it who wrote the letter. In a friendly letter, usually only the first name is given.

(heading)	July 8, _____
(greeting)	Dear Jenny,
(body)	I am so happy that your parents will let you come visit me soon. Nothing has been the same since you moved away. Everyone that I meet, I compare to you. You were and still are my best friend. It'll be great to see you. I can hardly wait.
(closing)	Your best friend,
(signature)	Polly

The **business letter** is similar in most respects to the friendly letter; however, it is more formal, more information is usually given, and it also includes an inside address. The parts of a business letter follow:

Heading: The heading includes the writer's address and the date.

Inside address: The inside address includes the title of the person to whom the letter is being sent and his or her address.

Greeting: The greeting is more formal in a business letter than in a friendly letter. The greeting includes the name and title of the person receiving the letter. If the name or title of the person is not known, the person may be addressed in the greeting as *Dear Sir* or *Dear Madam*. The greeting, which is followed by a colon (:), is placed below the inside address.

Body: The body of a business letter, like the body of a friendly letter, contains the message and is the main part of the letter. However, the body of a business letter is written more formally.

Student Study Pages *continued*

Closing: The closing of a business letter is more formal than the closing of a friendly letter. The most common closings are *Sincerely yours, Sincerely, Yours truly,* or *Cordially.* The closing is followed by a comma (,).

Signature: The signature of a business letter is more formal than that of a friendly letter. It usually includes your whole name, and it is handwritten. The signature is below the closing.

(heading)   23 Linden Lane
                          Princeton, New Jersey 08540
                          January 11, _____

(inside address) Dr. James Holmes, President
                          Instruments, Inc.
                          456 Nassau Street
                          Princeton, New Jersey 08540

(greeting)   Dear Dr. Holmes:

(body)   Last May, I ordered a pocket calculator from your company. The calculator arrived in June, but I still have not been able to use it because it arrived missing a part. I immediately phoned to inform your company about this, but everyone I spoke to told me to write a letter to your company explaining my problem. I wrote six letters to your company, and to this date, no one has replied. As a result, I am writing to you, the president of the company.

I would like you to find out why no one has answered any of my letters. If I do not hear from you in a short period of time, I intend to write to the Better Business Bureau.

(closing)   Yours truly,

(signature)   *Jane Smith*
                          Jane Smith

Special Notes

Business letters today are mostly written with the two addresses, the closing, and the signature flush left. The first sentence of each paragraph in a business letter usually is not indented and is flush left. Paragraphs are separated by adding an extra space between them. In a typed business letter, the typed name is usually below the handwritten signature.

Student Study Pages *continued*

Friendly letters, which are usually handwritten, may also be written in this way. In most friendly letters, however, the first sentence of each paragraph is indented and the closing and signature are placed under the date to the right.

The envelope should always have a return address. The return address is usually placed in the upper left-hand corner of the envelope. The return address should include your name and address. In the center of the envelope, write the complete address of the person to whom you are writing. Here is a sample envelope. Notice that the following information is given:

- The name appears at the top.
- The street address is next.
- The city, state, and zip code appear on the bottom line.

Jane Doe
111 Love Lane
Anywhere, CA 92123

John Doe
123 Sherman Rd.
Anywhere, CA 92123

66

Name _____

Practice 1

Directions: Here are ten topics for a three- or four-page composition. Write the letter *N* if the topic is too narrow, the letter *B* if the topic is too broad, and the letter *M* if the topic is manageable.

_____ 1. The automobile industry

_____ 2. North America

_____ 3. America

_____ 4. Chicago

_____ 5. Horse racing

_____ 6. Definition of language

_____ 7. An example of propaganda

_____ 8. A comparison of the habits of the gorilla with those of the baboon

_____ 9. A comparison of the lives of two famous presidents

_____ 10. Education in the 19th century

Name_____

Practice 2

Directions: Below are three topics that are too narrow for a three- or four-page composition. Enlarge each topic into a broader topic.

> **Sample:** Foods I Like to Eat—The Importance of a Well-Balanced Diet to Health

1. Description of a Whale

_____

_____

2. My Feelings Toward School Dances

_____

_____

3. My Favorite Fad

_____

_____

Name_____

Practice 3

Directions: Below are three broad topics. Narrow each topic into a more manageable one for a three- or four-page composition.

Sample: Television—A Comparison of Three Current Television Situation Comedies

1. Reptiles

    _____

    _____

2. Actors

    _____

    _____

3. Science

    _____

    _____

Name _____

Practice 4

Directions: Below are five topics. Write the letter *N* next to the topic if it is too narrow or the letter *B* if it is too broad. Then, write a manageable topic for a three- or four-page composition.

1. Space Movies _____

_____

_____

2. The Composition of an Aquarium _____

_____

_____

3. What My Name Means _____

_____

_____

4. Description of a Monarch Butterfly _____

_____

_____

5. An Exposé of Racketeering _____

_____

_____

Name _____

Practice 5

Directions: Choose a sentence from each group that makes the best topic sentence for each topic. Then explain why you made that choice.

Group I

A Comparison of School Life in Colonial Times with That of Today

    a. It must have been fun to go to school in colonial times.
    b. I wouldn't have wanted to go to school in colonial times.
    c. Going to school in colonial times was difficult.
    d. Schools have changed significantly.
    e. Schools today have greatly changed from schools in colonial times.

_____

_____

_____

_____

Group II

How I Spend My Summer Vacations

    a. Summer is the best time of the year for me.
    b. I like to loaf around in the summer.
    c. Summer vacations are those I look forward to all year long.
    d. The way I spend my summer vacation varies each year.
    e. Summer vacations are too short.

_____

_____

_____

_____

Name _____

Practice 6

Directions: Write a topic sentence for the first paragraph in a composition on the following topics.

1. A Comparison of the Worst and Best Teachers I Have Had in My Life

_____

_____

_____

_____

2. A Comparison of Different Types of Family Situation Comedy
    Television Shows

_____

_____

_____

_____

Name_____

Practice 7

Directions: Write a topic sentence for the first paragraph in a composition on the following topics.

1. Choosing a Career

_____

_____

_____

_____

2. Life in the World of Robots

_____

_____

_____

_____

Name_____

Practice 8

Directions: Write an introductory paragraph for a composition concerning your childhood. Choose a title for it. Write a topic sentence that will attract your reader's attention.

_____

_____

_____

_____

_____

_____

_____

_____

_____

_____

_____

_____

_____

_____

_____

_____

_____

Name_____

Practice 9

Directions: Write an introductory paragraph for a composition on the following topic: "The Person I Would Most Like to Be."

_____

_____

_____

_____

_____

_____

_____

_____

_____

_____

_____

_____

_____

_____

_____

_____

Name_____

Practice 10

Directions: Write an introductory paragraph for a composition on the following topic: "My Life as a Space Traveler."

_____

_____

_____

_____

_____

_____

_____

_____

_____

_____

_____

_____

_____

_____

_____

_____

Name_____

Practice 11

Directions: Write an introductory paragraph for a composition on the following topic: "How I Became an Olympic Champion."

_____

_____

_____

_____

_____

_____

_____

_____

_____

_____

_____

_____

_____

_____

_____

_____

Name _____

Practice 12

Directions: Write a concluding paragraph for a composition on the following topic: "My Life as an Actor."

_____

_____

_____

_____

_____

_____

_____

_____

_____

_____

_____

_____

_____

_____

_____

_____

_____

© Good Apple GA13058

Name_____

Practice 13

Directions: Write a concluding paragraph for a composition concerning your early childhood.

_____

_____

_____

_____

_____

_____

_____

_____

_____

_____

_____

_____

_____

_____

_____

Name _____

Practice 14

Directions: Choose a topic. Limit the topic, state a central idea for it, and then state your feelings about it. List some possible items that you want to discuss.

General topic:

_____

_____

Limited topic:

_____

_____

Central idea:

_____

_____

Author's feelings:

_____

_____

List of possible items to discuss:

_____

_____

Name _____

Practice 15

Directions: Choose a topic. Limit the topic, state a central idea for it, and then state your feelings about it. List some possible items that you want to discuss. Decide on those that are equal in importance. List these together. Divide these main topics into subtopics. Then write a composition on another sheet of paper so that each main topic is a paragraph and the subtopics are part of the supporting details.

_____

_____

_____

_____

_____

_____

_____

_____

_____

_____

_____

_____

_____

_____

_____

Name _____

Practice 16

Directions: By using the following letter as an example, write a friendly letter to a friend or relative. Use a separate sheet of paper for your letter.

172 Rogers Avenue
Logan, Iowa 55555
March 10, _____

Dear _____,

    Your visit is going to be the most exciting event of the year. The whole family is going to come to a picnic in our backyard, and we'll have fried chicken and blueberry pie.

    I can hardly wait for you to come. You'll be sleeping in my room. I can show you my photo album, and you can play with my dog, Rusty. Come soon!

Your cousin,

_____

Name _____

Practice 17

Directions: By using the following letter as an example, write a thank-you letter to a friend or member of your family. Use a separate sheet of paper for your letter.

December 2, _____

Dear _____,

    I want to tell you how much I enjoyed the picture that you made for me! It is simply lovely. I brought it in immediately to have it framed, and it is now hanging in my room.

    Please give my love to everyone. We are all looking forward to seeing you at the family reunion.

Love,

_____

Name _____

Practice 18

Directions: By using the following invitation as an example, write an informal invitation to one of your friends. Use a separate sheet of paper for your letter.

Room 101
Eaton Elementary School
April 3, _____

Dear Mr. and Mrs. _____,

Our class is presenting a play in our classroom on April 20 from 1:30 to 2:30. We would be pleased to have you come.

Sincerely yours,

Mrs. Jones's Class

84

Name _____

Practice 19

Directions: By using the following letter as an example, pretend to write a business letter to a company to order something from them. Use a separate sheet of paper for your letter.

1571 Conrad Avenue
Brockley, California 94501

July 9, _____

Mary Spero, Parts Supervisor
Jones Electrical Company
932 Railing Avenue
Oakland, California 94604

Dear Ms. Spero:

The ABC Corporation in Brockley informs me that you stock the LT-0140 tube for the 1999 model television set manufactured by Grant. The model number is RBC-143V67.

Since the tube is easily replaced, ABC has suggested that I order it from you by mail. My check for the cost of the tube plus mailing is enclosed. Please send it to the above address.

Yours truly,

Peter Potts

Peter Potts

Section 3

OUTLINING

Explanation

Although outlines are most often used to sketch the contents of long, complex papers before the actual writing begins, they are also useful in the development of shorter papers and even paragraphs. An outline forces the writer to stop and think about the way that he or she will organize ideas and controls any urge to follow a train of thought beyond the limits of the paper. Help students recognize that good writers are good thinkers; that is, their writing is organized and logical.

Main Topic

In outlining, the main topic is of prime importance. It helps join together everything grouped under it. Because of the importance of the main topic in an outline, it is usually "signaled" with a Roman numeral (I, II, III, and so on), and the first word is capitalized. For example:

    I. Main topic

Subtopics and Details

Subtopics in an outline are grouped under and are related to the main topics. Each subtopic expresses some idea or information about the main topic. To show that subtopics are related to the main topics, indent them under the main topics. Each subtopic is signaled by a capital letter (A, B, C, D, and so on), and the first word is capitalized. For example:

    I. Main topic

        A. Prime importance

        B. Signaled by a Roman numeral (I, II, III, and so on)

        C. Begins with a capital letter

You can include more details in your outline by grouping them below the appropriate subtopics. These details are represented by Arabic numerals (1, 2, 3, 4, and so on), and the first word is capitalized. For example:

OUTLINING

II. Subtopics
  A. Grouped under main topics
  B. Related to main topics
    1. Indented under main topic
    2. Signaled by a capital letter (A, B, C, D, and so on)
    3. Begins with a capital letter

III. Specific details
  A. Grouped under appropriate subtopics
  B. Represented by Arabic numerals (1, 2, 3, 4, and so on)

You can include even more specific details in your outline by grouping them below the appropriate Arabic numerals. These details are represented by lowercase letters (a, b, c, d, and so on), and the first word is capitalized. For example:

IV. More specific details
  A. Grouped under appropriate Arabic numerals
  B. Represented by lowercase letters (a, b, c, d, and so on)

Special Note

To include even more specific details under the lowercase a, b, c, d, and so on, indent and use Arabic numerals in parentheses.

Here is an example of an outline that includes the main topic, subtopics, specific details, and more specific details.

(main topic)	I. The dictionary	
(subtopics)	A. An important reference tool	
	B. Uses of the dictionary	
(specific detail)	1. Information concerning a word	
(more specific details)	a. Spelling	
	b. Definitions	
	c. Correct usage	
	d. Syllabication	
(specific detail)	2. Other useful information	
(more specific details)	a. Biographical entries	
	b. Signs and symbols	
	c. Forms of address	

© Good Apple GA13058

87

OUTLINING

There are two types of outlines—a topic outline and a sentence outline. Before constructing an outline, students should decide which kind they will use. A topic outline consists of words and phrases and is useful in preparing short or long papers. A sentence outline consists of complete sentences and is used primarily in preparing long papers.

Learning Objectives

Students should be able to:

- choose a word or phrase from the word list that best describes each group of words.
- arrange a list of words in a number of different ways and write the common characteristic of each group.
- choose the word from each group of words that does not belong.
- write a main topic for a given groups of words.
- write the main topic of a given paragraph.
- place the correct subtopic under each main topic.
- organize a list of words into a main topic and subtopics.
- write a possible title for a paragraph.
- write the main topic and subtopic of a paragraph in topic or sentence outline form.
- place subtopics and details under their correct main topics.
- write an outline of a paragraph in topic or sentence outline form.

Directions for Student Study Pages and Practices

Use the student pages (pages 90–105) to help students acquire, reinforce, and review outlining. Make copies of the reproducible Student Study Pages on pages 90 and 91 for each student. This section can be used as a reference while students do the practices, as well as when they do their own writing.

Pick and choose the practices based on the needs and developmental levels of your students. Answers for the student practice pages are reproducible, so you may choose to give your students the practice pages as well as the answer pages to progress on their own. The answers are on pages 115–119.

Extensions

■ Students can choose short pieces from newspapers or magazines and make short outlines for the authors' works. This way they can see how they may have been written.

■ Write a central idea on the board with an outline form below it. Fill in various parts of the outline and ask students to fill in the empty spaces with ideas for the story.

■ Divide the group into teams. Give each team a sheet of paper. Ask for one volunteer to begin by writing a topic at the top of the paper. The paper is then passed around and each student adds other main topics and subtopics to come up with an outline for a coherent story.

Name _____

Student Study Pages

Outlining

Main Topic

In **outlining**, the main topic is of prime importance. It helps join together everything grouped under it. Because of the importance of the main topic in an outline, it is usually "signaled" with a Roman numeral (I, II, III, and so on), and the first word is capitalized. For example:

I. The dictionary

Subtopics and Details

Subtopics in an outline are grouped under and are related to the main topics. Each subtopic expresses some idea or information about the main topic. To show that subtopics are related to the main topics, indent them under the main topic. Each subtopic is signaled by a capital letter (A, B, C, D, and so on), and the first word is capitalized. For example:

I. The dictionary
    A. An important reference tool
    B. Uses of the dictionary

You can include more **details** in your outline by grouping them below the appropriate subtopics. These details are represented by Arabic numerals (1, 2, 3, 4, and so on), and the first word is capitalized. For example:

I. The dictionary
    A. An important reference tool
    B. Uses of the dictionary
        1. Information concerning a word
        2. Other useful information

You can include even **more specific details** in your outline by grouping them below the appropriate Arabic numerals. These details are represented by lowercase letters (a, b, c, d, and so on), and the first word is capitalized. For example:

I. The dictionary
    A. An important reference tool
    B. Uses of the dictionary
        1. Information concerning a word
            a. Spelling
            b. Definitions
            c. Correct usage
            d. Syllabication

Student Study Pages *continued*

    2. Other useful information
       a. Biographical information
       b. Signs and symbols
       c. Forms of address

To include even more specific details under the lowercase a, b, c, d, and so on, indent and use Arabic numerals in parentheses.

Special Note

There are two types of outlines—a topic outline and a sentence outline. Before constructing an outline, you should decide which kind you will use. A topic outline consists of words and phrases and is useful in preparing short or long papers. A sentence outline consists of complete sentences and is used primarily in preparing long papers.

Use the skeleton outline below as an example as you write your own outlines.

  I. _____

    A. _____

      1. _____

      2. _____

    B. _____

      1. _____

        a. _____

        b. _____

      2. _____

        a. _____

        b. _____

Name _____

Practice 1

Directions: First, find what the items in each group have in common, and then choose a word or phrase from the list below that best describes the group. You will not use all the words and phrases.

> **Words and phrases:** books, fiction books, nonfiction books, fruit, vegetables, food, cooked food, desserts, dairy products, long books, writing, fowl, animals, tame animals, female animals, wood, wood products, meat, beef, pork, lamb

1. pears, apples, bananas _____

2. meat, tomatoes, apples _____

3. milk, cheese, butter _____

4. jello, applesauce, ice cream _____

5. liver, pork chops, lamb chops _____

6. sow, mare, doe _____

7. biography, autobiography, novel _____

8. biography, autobiography, dictionary _____

9. novel, comics, fairy tale _____

10. paper, telephone pole, furniture _____

Name_____

Practice 2

Directions: Read the word list carefully. Then place the words into groups according to a common feature. State the common feature for each group. For example, *pear* can come under the more specific category of *fruit* or the more general category of *food*.

> **Word List:** pear, car, raisins, barley, trains, ships, gliders, planes, apples, prunes, oats, wheat, trucks, canoes, peach, eggs, butter, banana, orange, cheese

_____

_____

_____

_____

Name _____

Practice 3

Directions: Read the word list carefully. Then place the words into ten groups according to common features. State the common feature for each group.

> **Word List:** small, wood, brass, round, silk, oil, wheat, hexagon, stockings, tin, skim, triangle, wool, satin, meter, coal, nylon, booties, gram, iron, rectangle, barley, socks, octagon, scan, oats, liter, oval, minute, mammoth, survey, cylindrical, huge

1. _____

   _____

2. _____

   _____

3. _____

   _____

4. _____

   _____

5. _____

   _____

6. _____

   _____

7. _____

   _____

8. _____

   _____

9. _____

   _____

10. _____

94

Name_____

Practice 4

Directions: Read each set of words carefully. Circle the word from each set that does not belong and briefly explain why it does not belong.

1. schnauzer, angora, spitz, collie

   _____

2. pine, fern, poplar, spruce

   _____

3. hobby, post, position, job

   _____

4. fly, butterfly, termite, tick

   _____

5. stag, sire, drake, ram

   _____

6. trout, clams, oysters, lobster

   _____

7. sword, scythe, saw, lance

   _____

8. cape, sweater, vest, poncho

   _____

9. mammoth, dinosaur, rhinoceros, dodo

   _____

10. octagon, hexagon, polygon, triangle

   _____

Name_____

Practice 5

Directions: Read each set of words carefully. Circle the word from each set that does not belong and briefly explain why it does not belong.

1. lad, tomboy, chap, guy

   _____

2. puddle, river, lake, pond

   _____

3. pouch, bag, drawer, purse

   _____

4. biography, math textbook, autobiography, novel

   _____

5. lawyer, counselor, attorney, prosecutor

   _____

6. shears, knife, saw, pliers

   _____

7. quart, gallon, liter, bowl

   _____

8. centigrade, fahrenheit, Kelvin, faraday

   _____

9. arc, line, circle, curve

   _____

10. bit, byte, disk, book

   _____

Name_____

Practice 6

Directions: Read each set of words carefully. Circle the word from each set that does not belong and briefly explain why it does not belong.

1. effect, help, result, outcome

_____

2. game, sport, fun, animal

_____

3. magnificent, superb, palatial, popular

_____

4. malice, mire, grudge, spite

_____

5. charge, defy, challenge, dare

_____

6. slander, defame, devastate, malign

_____

7. booty, shoe, plunder, spoil

_____

8. falcon, eagle, canary, hawk

_____

9. grasshopper, termite, fly, scorpion

_____

10. mean, median, mode, range

_____

Name_____

Practice 7

Directions: Write one main topic for each group of words below.

1. California, Oregon, Washington

   _____

2. pecan, almond, walnut

   _____

3. ship, train, plane

   _____

4. Pontiac, Buick, Ford

   _____

5. Delicious, Winesap, McIntosh

   _____

6. Woodrow Wilson, Theodore Roosevelt, Dwight D. Eisenhower

   _____

7. Betsy Ross, Florence Nightingale, Joan of Arc

   _____

8. elephant, rhinoceros, hippopotamus

   _____

9. chicken, donkey, pig

   _____

10. hammer, pliers, wrench

   _____

Name _____

Practice 8

Directions: Read the following two paragraphs carefully. Write a possible title for each.

Animals may be divided into two groups: *cold-blooded*, such as reptiles and fish, and *warm-blooded*, including birds and mammals. The terms for these groups are not well chosen, because cold-blooded animals sometimes have a body temperature higher than warm-blooded animals. A lizard sitting on a rock in the sun of a warm summer day may have a body temperature as high as that of a person with a very high fever. The same lizard at night, however, will have a temperature far below that of a person. At both extremes of external temperature, a human's temperature is almost constant.

1. _____

_____

The heart of a turtle, a cold-blooded animal, is especially hardy and can easily be kept beating for many hours after its removal from the body. Not only does the removed heart continue to contract, but—even more remarkable—its beat is regular. Close observation shows that the pattern of contraction is the same as that of an unremoved heart.

2. _____

_____

99

Name _____

Practice 9

Directions: Below are groups of words with main topics. Place the correct subtopic under each main topic.

1. Atlanta, Oregon, Washington, Tulsa, San Diego, Maine, Arizona, Newark

    I. States

        A. _____

        B. _____

        C. _____

        D. _____

    II. Cities

        A. _____

        B. _____

        C. _____

        D. _____

2. China, South America, England, United States, Asia, France, North America, Africa

    I. Continents

        A. _____

        B. _____

        C. _____

        D. _____

    II. Countries

        A. _____

        B. _____

        C. _____

        D. _____

3. Deer, bear, marlin, trout, whale, goldfish, cat, tuna

    I. Mammals

        A. _____

        B. _____

        C. _____

        D. _____

    II. Fish

        A. _____

        B. _____

        C. _____

        D. _____

Name_____

Practice 10

Directions: Below are groups of words with main topics. Place the correct subtopic under each main topic.

1. California, Oregon, Maine, New Hampshire, Connecticut, Massachusetts, Washington

   I. Eastern states   II. Western states

      A. _____   A. _____

      B. _____   B. _____

      C. _____   C. _____

      D. _____

2. Fly, rattler, asp, cobra, louse, grasshopper, beetle

   I. Snakes   II. Insects

      A. _____   A. _____

      B. _____   B. _____

      C. _____   C. _____

                                       D. _____

3. Dog, tiger, leopard, cat, elephant, giraffe, hamster, turtle

   I. Domesticated animals   II. Wild animals

      A. _____   A. _____

      B. _____   B. _____

      C. _____   C. _____

                                       D. _____

Name _____

Practice 11

Directions: Read the word list carefully. Then choose the main topics and list the correct subtopics under the main topics. Your main topics and subtopics should fit the given skeleton outlines.

> **Word List:** paramecium, evergreens, snakes, fir, lizards, hemlocks, junipers, turtles, pines, reptiles, amoeba, yews, one-celled organisms

1. I. _____

    A. _____

    B _____

    C. _____

    D. _____

    E. _____

2. I. _____

    A. _____

    B. _____

    C. _____

3. I. _____

    A. _____

    B. _____

Name_____

Practice 12

Directions: Read the following paragraph carefully. Then write, in outline form, its main topic and subtopics. Choose the type of outline you will use. Then use the same form throughout. **Hint:** Your outline can either be in words and phrases (topic outline) or in sentences (sentence outline). Remember to be consistent.

Indentured servants were used in all colonies to overcome the labor shortage problem. Ship captains brought poverty-stricken boys, girls, men, and women to America. The ship captains collected fares from each of their passengers, as well as money from whomever would agree to take on an individual as an indentured servant. The indentured servant, in turn, agreed to work for room, board, and clothing for four to seven years until the debt was paid.

I. _____

   A. _____

   B. _____

   C. _____

   D. _____

Name_____

Practice 13

Directions: Below are words and groups of words. First find the main topics. Then place the correct subtopic and details under each main topic.

> **Word List:** hawk, songbirds, falcon, asp, cobra, birds of prey, snakes, sparrow, turtles, birds, canary, eagle, lizards, reptiles

I. _____

   A. _____

   B. _____

   C. _____

      1. _____

      2. _____

II. _____

   A. _____

      1. _____

      2. _____

      3. _____

   B. _____

      1. _____

      2. _____

Name_____

Practice 14

Directions: Read the following paragraph carefully. Then write a title and an outline for it. State whether your outline is a topic or sentence outline.

Walter Reed, a United States Army doctor, is credited with determining that yellow fever is transmitted by the bite of a mosquito. He used controlled experiments to prove his theory and to disprove that yellow fever is spread by such things as bedding and clothing that had been used by a yellow fever victim. Once he was able to prove his theory, the battle against yellow fever was almost won. As a means of conquering yellow fever, the mosquito that carried this dread disease was isolated and wiped out.

_____

_____

_____

_____

_____

_____

_____

_____

_____

Student's Name _____

Assessment Tool Progress Report

Progress

_____

_____

_____

_____

_____

Improvement

_____

_____

_____

_____

_____

Comments

_____

_____

_____

_____

_____

Diagnostic Checklist for General and Practical Aspects of Writing

Student's Name _____

Grade _____

Teacher _____

Paragraphs	Yes	No	Sometimes
The student is able to:			
1. develop a paragraph using different kinds of details such as examples, comparison/contrast, cause and effect, description, and definition.			
2. write a group of paragraphs on a topic.			
3. express ideas clearly.			
4. express ideas logically.			
5. present ideas creatively.			
6. revise a paragraph.			
7. proofread a paragraph.			

Composition	Yes	No	Sometimes
The student is able to:			
1. choose a manageable topic to write about.			
2. write the topic sentence for the opening paragraph.			
3. write an opening paragraph.			
4. write a concluding paragraph.			
5. write a composition.			
6. revise a composition.			
7. proofread a composition.			

**Diagnostic Checklist for General
and Practical Aspects of Writing** *continued*

Letter Writing

	Yes	No	Sometimes
The student is able to:			
1. write a friendly letter.			
2. write a thank-you letter.			
3. write an invitation.			
4. write the five parts of a friendly letter.			
5. address an envelope for a friendly letter, including the zip code.			
6. write a business letter using appropriate language.			
7. write the six parts of a business letter.			
8. order something by mail.			
9. write information in a concise manner.			
10. write a letter of complaint.			
11. write a letter of apology.			
12. address a business envelope, including the zip code.			

Outlining

	Yes	No	Sometimes
The student is able to:			
1. make discriminations.			

2. classify objects:
  a. put things together that belong together
  b. group things into categories			

3. use outlines for reporting information.			
4. use Roman numerals for the main topics.			
5. put a period after each Roman numeral.			

Diagnostic Checklist for General and Practical Aspects of Writing *continued*

The student is able to:	Yes	No	Sometimes
6. use capital letters for subtopics.			
7. indent subtopics.			
8. use ordinary Arabic numerals for details under subtopics.			
9. use small letters under the details for more specific details.			
10. put a period after each number and letter.			
11. begin each topic with a capital letter.			

Answers

Writing Paragraphs

Practice 1 (page 25)

(Sample Answers)

1. Reasons why living in a spaceship for three months was difficult.
   Topic: Living in a spaceship
2. Reasons and examples why my best friend is always very lucky.
   Topic: The luck of my best friend
3. Reasons why no one could anticipate the consequences of John's actions.
   Topic: The consequences of John's actions
4. An explanation and examples of both good moments and bad moments that a child of divorced parents experiences.
   Topic: Being the child of divorced parents
5. Reasons why my first-grade teacher was the best teacher I ever had.
   Topic: My first-grade teacher

Practice 2 (page 26)

Answers will vary.

Practice 3 (page 27)

(Sample Answers)

1. Many, many years ago there lived a giant Cormorant who was the terror of all the countryside.
2. All the countryfolk were greatly alarmed about the slaughtering.

Practice 4 (page 28)

(Sample Answers)

1. Jack, a very brave boy, decided that he would rid the countryside of this dreadful monster.
2. The countryfolk were grateful that Jack freed the countryside of the giant.

Practice 5 (page 29)

Paragraphs will vary.

Practice 6 (page 30)

Paragraphs will vary.

Practice 7 (page 31)

Paragraphs will vary.

Practice 8 (page 32)

Sentence order: 5, 6, 2, 1, 3, 4 or 5, 6, 1, 3, 4, 2

Practice 9 (page 33)

Sentence order: 6, 2, 7, 1, 5, 4, 3

Practice 10 (pages 34 and 35)

Group I Sentence order: 6, 1, 5, 2, 4, 3
Group II Sentence order: 2, 5, 3, 4, 1
Group III Sentence order: 3, 1, 4, 6, 5, 2 or 3, 4, 1, 6, 5, 2

Practice 11 (page 36)

Sentence order: 5, 8, 7, 2, 4, 1, 9, 6, 3, 10

Practice 12 (page 37)

(Sample Answer)

We wonder what the mystery is.

Practice 13 (page 38)

(Sample Answer)

Jake doesn't know what to do to convince his mother to allow him to try out for the team.

Practice 14 (page 39)

(Sample Answer)

After a short while, we were off to try our luck at the lake.

Practice 15 (page 40)

(Sample Answer)

What else could it have been but the cracks?

Practice 16 (page 41)

(Sample Answer)

 Television commercials rely very heavily on propaganda techniques to get people to buy their products. Although there are a number of propaganda techniques that commercials use, the one that is most often used is that of "getting on the bandwagon." When commercials use "getting on the bandwagon," they try to make people feel left out if they don't buy the advertised product. Since most people do not like to feel that they are the only ones without something, this technique is very successful. Television commercials must be successful since so much money is spent on them.

Practice 17 (page 42)

(Sample Answer)

 Going to a new school is a traumatic experience for any student. There are so many adjustments you have to make, and so many new things you have to learn. For example, you are the outsider, and you are afraid of doing or saying anything

Practice 17 (page 42) *continued*

wrong, because if you do, you will not be accepted. Everyone seems to know everyone else except you. Also, you know that everyone is looking you over, so you have to always be on guard. It's very difficult being a new student—something I'd like to avoid.

Practice 18 (page 43)

(Sample Answer)

Television commercials can have some dire effects on young children. Young children seem to be especially attracted to television commercials. It wouldn't be far off to say that television commercials seem to mesmerize children. Have you ever noticed how children will stop whatever they are doing the moment a television commercial comes on? Television commercials get children's attention so that they can sell them lots of things. Children pressure their parents to buy them the advertised products. Unfortunately, many of the advertised products do not live up to the advertisements. As a result, many children eventually become cynical. The television industry should try to be more responsible in advertising aimed toward young children. They should realize that the cynical children of today will become the cynical adults of tomorrow.

Practice 19 (page 44)

Paragraphs will vary.

Practice 20 (page 45)

Paragraphs will vary.

Practice 21 (page 46)

Paragraphs will vary.

Practice 22 (page 47)

(Sample Answer)

In high school and college, Brett's one goal was athletic success so that he could be in the Olympics. Brett's goal to be in the Olympics became such an obsession that he could not do anything that did not directly or indirectly relate to achieving his goal. He practiced for hours every day. He exercised, ate well, and slept at least eight hours every night. Throughout school, Brett allowed nothing and no one to deter him from his goal.

Practice 23 (page 48)

(Sample Answer)

Ben Simpson was all dressed up because he was going to a party for his friend, Carol Anne. Ben had a great birthday gift for Carol Anne. It was a brand-new video game. Ben actually wanted the gift for himself, but he knew if he gave the gift to Carol Anne, he would be able to use it, too.

Practice 24 (page 49)

Our English assignments are never very interesting ones. For example, at the beginning of the term, we write on "How We Spent Our Summer Vacation," and after the winter break, we write on "How We Spent Our Winter Break." For Mother's Day, we write on "What Is Special About a Member of Our Family." At the end of the term, we write on "How We Intend to Spend Our Summer Vacation." I wonder how teachers can be so unimaginative!

Practice 25 (page 50)

The Pilgrim child's life in school wasn't very easy. He or she usually had strict teachers who were men. When a child whispered in school, he or she was severely punished. The punishment usually consisted of wearing the whispering stick. This was a piece of wood that the child had to hold inside his or her mouth. There was a string at each end, which was tied behind his or her neck. Pilgrim children were also subjected to many whippings. I'm sure everyone is glad he or she is going to school today rather than a long time ago.

Writing a Composition

Practice 1 (page 67)

1. B 2. B 3. B 4. B 5. B 6. N 7. N 8. M 9. M 10. B

Practice 2 (page 68)

(Sample Answers)

1. The Life and Habits of a Whale
2. My Feelings Toward School-Sponsored Functions
3. Fads and Their Effect on Your Social Life

Practice 3 (page 69)

(Sample Answers)

1. The Life and Habits of the Cobra and the Asp
2. A Comparison of the Careers of My Two Favorite Actors
3. The Contributions That Space Travel Has Made to Society

Practice 4 (page 70)

(Sample Answers)

1. B; A Comparison of My Two Favorite Space Movies
2. N; How to Stock and Maintain an Aquarium
3. N; A Study of the Meanings of the Most Popular Names
4. N; The Life and Habits of Some Insects
5. B; An Exposé of Racketeering in the 1970s

Practice 5 (page 71)

Group I. e. This sentence is the most closely related to the topic. It also gives the most information about what follows.

Group II. d. The reasons are the same as those for Group I.

Practice 6 (page 72)

(Sample Answers)

1. It is easier for me to write about the worst teacher I have had than to write about the best, because memories of the former have been permanently burned into my brain.
2. Family situation comedy shows ranging from the outright slapstick to the more sophisticated appeal to different types of audiences.

Practice 7 (page 73)

(Sample Answers)

1. One of the most difficult decisions I must make in my life is deciding on a career.
2. Life as a human being in the world of robots can have its problems as well as its rewards.

Practice 8 (page 74)

Paragraphs will vary.

Practice 9 (page 75)

Paragraphs will vary.

Practice 10 (page 76)

Paragraphs will vary.

Practice 11 (page 77)

Paragraphs will vary.

Practice 12 (page 78)

Paragraphs will vary.

Practice 13 (page 79)

Paragraphs will vary.

Practice 14 (page 80)

Answers will vary.

Practice 15 (page 81)

Answers will vary.

Practice 16 (page 82)

Letters will vary.

Practice 17 (page 83)

Letters will vary.

Practice 18 (page 84)

Letters will vary.

Practice 19 (page 85)

Letters will vary.

Outlining

Practice 1 (page 92)

1. fruit
2. food
3. dairy products
4. desserts
5. meat
6. female animals
7. books
8. nonfiction books
9. fiction books
10. wood products

Practice 2 (page 93)

(Sample Answers)

1. Fruits—pear, raisins, apples, prunes, peach, banana, orange
2. Dried fruits—raisins, prunes
3. Grains—barley, oats, wheat
4. Food—pear, raisins, barley, apples, prunes, oats, wheat, peach, banana, orange, eggs, butter, cheese
5. Dairy products—eggs, butter, cheese
6. Transportation—car, trains, ships, gliders, planes, trucks, canoes
7. Land transportation—car, trains, trucks
8. Water transportation—ships, canoes
9. Air transportation—gliders, planes

Practice 3 (page 94)

(Sample Answers)

1. Fuels—wood, oil, coal
2. Metals—brass, tin, iron
3. Fabrics—silk, wool, satin, nylon

Practice 3 (page 94) *continued*

 4. Shapes—round, cylindrical, oval, triangle, hexagon, rectangle, octagon
 5. Grains—wheat, barley, oats
 6. Footwear—stockings, booties, socks
 7. Fast reading—skim, scan, survey
 8. Metric terms—meter, gram, liter
 9. Geometric figures—hexagon, triangle, rectangle, octagon
10. Sizes—small, huge, mammoth, minute

Practice 4 (page 95)

(Sample Answers)

 1. angora (not a dog)
 2. poplar (not an evergreen)
 3. hobby (not a vocation, it's an avocation)
 4. tick (not an insect—a tick has eight legs)
 5. drake (not four-legged)
 6. trout (not a shellfish)
 7. lance (used for ramming or piercing, like an arrow)
 8. sweater (has sleeves)
 9. rhinoceros (not extinct)
10. polygon (too general)

Practice 5 (page 96)

(Sample Answers)

 1. tomboy (not a male)
 2. river (flowing water)
 3. drawer (not carried)
 4. novel (a fiction book)
 5. prosecutor (too specific—a special kind of attorney)
 6. pliers (used for gripping, not cutting)
 7. bowl (not a liquid measure)
 8. faraday (not a degree of temperature)
 9. line (not curved)
10. book (not a computer term)

Practice 6 (page 97)

(Sample Answers)

 1. help (different meaning than others—not an end)
 2. animal (not an amusement)
 3. popular (different meaning than others)
 4. mire (different meaning than others—means "deep mud or slush")
 5. charge (different meaning than others—means "to accuse")
 6. devastate (different meaning than others—means "to bring to ruin")

Practice 6 (page 97) *continued*

7. shoe (not rich gains taken from others)
8. canary (not a bird of prey)
9. scorpion (not an insect—a scorpion has eight legs)
10. range (not a measure of central tendency)

Practice 7 (page 98)

(Sample Answers)

1. Western states
2. Nuts
3. Modes of transportation
4. Makes of cars
5. Kinds of apples
6. U.S. presidents
7. Famous women
8. Thick-skinned animals
9. Farm animals
10. Tools

Practice 8 (page 99)

(Sample Answers)

1. Cold-Blooded and Warm-Blooded Animals
2. The Heart of a Turtle

Practice 9 (page 100)

1. I. States
   A. Oregon
   B. Washington
   C. Maine
   D. Arizona
   II. Cities
   A. Atlanta
   B. Tulsa
   C. San Diego
   D. Newark

2. I. Continents
   A. South America
   B. Asia
   C. North America
   D. Africa
   II. Countries
   A. China
   B. England
   C. United States
   D. France

3. I. Mammals
   A. Deer
   B. Bear
   C. Whale
   D. Cat
   II. Fish
   A. Marlin
   B. Trout
   C. Goldfish
   D. Tuna

Practice 10 (page 101)

1. I. Eastern states
   A. Maine
   B. New Hampshire
   C. Connecticut
   D. Massachusetts

   II. Western states
   A. California
   B. Oregon
   C. Washington

2. I. Snakes
   A. Rattler
   B. Asp
   C. Cobra

   II. Insects
   A. Fly
   B. Louse
   C. Grasshopper
   D. Beetle

3. I. Domesticated animals
   A. Dog
   B. Cat
   C. Hamster
   D. Turtle

   II. Wild animals
   A. Tiger
   B. Leopard
   C. Elephant
   D. Giraffe

Practice 11 (page 102)

1. I. Evergreens
   A. Fir
   B. Hemlocks
   C. Junipers
   D. Pines
   E. Yews

2. I. Reptiles
   A. Snakes
   B. Lizards
   C. Turtles

3. I. One-Celled Organisms
   A. Paramecium
   B. Amoeba

Practice 12 (page 103)

(Sample sentence outline)

I. Indentured servants were used in the colonies.
   A. They were poverty-stricken persons.
   B. Ship captains brought them to America.
   C. They worked for room, board, and clothing.
   D. They worked from four to seven years.

Practice 13 (page 104)

I. Reptiles
   A. Turtles
   B. Lizards
   C. Snakes
      1. Asp
      2. Cobra

Practice 13 (page 104) *continued*

II. Birds
  A. Birds of prey
    1. Falcon
    2. Eagle
    3. Hawk
  B. Songbirds
    1. Sparrow
    2. Canary

Practice 14 (page 105)

(Sample topic outline)

Title: The Cause and Cure of Yellow Fever
  I. Walter Reed's experiments
    A. Disproves bedding and clothing theory
    B. Proves mosquito theory
  II. The conquering of yellow fever
    A. Isolating the mosquito
    B. Wiping out the mosquito

NOTES